A PROPER LITTLE NOORYEFF

Leonard Gregory

Published by the Press Syndicate of the University of Cambridge
The Pitt Building, Trumpington Street, Cambridge CB2 1RP
40 West 20th Street, New York, NY 10011–4211, USA
10 Stamford Road, Oakleigh, Victoria 3166, Australia

© Cambridge University Press 1992

First published 1992

Printed in Great Britain by
Greenshires Print Ltd, Kettering, Northamptonshire

A catalogue record for this book is available from the British Library

ISBN 0 521 42126 8

Performance
For permission to give a public performance of *A Proper Little Nooryeff* please write to Permissions Department, Cambridge University Press, The Edinburgh Building, Shaftesbury Road, Cambridge CB2 2RU.

Cover photograph by The Dance Library / Darryl Williams.

An educational hardback edition of the novel *A Proper Little Nooryeff* by Jean Ure is available in the New Windmills series from Heinemann Educational, published in January 1993 (SBN 435 12402 1).

GE

ABOUT THE PLAY

My introduction to ballet came at the age of twelve, when I was taken with a school party to a production of *Swan Lake*. Nobody had thought to prepare us for it, with the predictable result that all of us boys – I can't speak for the girls – were first amazed and then contemptuous at the sight of grown men leaping about the stage in tights. Our juvenile, yob-like reactions were very much akin to those of the Baboon and the Canary in the play – more suited to all-in wrestling than the genteel world of ballet.

In those days, most theatres of any size had miniature opera glasses mounted in holders on the backs of the seats, and by putting the grand sum of sixpence (or 2½p) in the slot, you could release them for use. Having quickly grown bored by the cavortings on stage, and having been warned beforehand against eating things, throwing things or starting any fights, I was soon seeking some other form of entertainment: the opera glasses caught my eye . . .

To begin with, as a matter of principle, I attempted to wrestle them out of the holder by brute force: this passed an agreeable quarter of an hour. Only when all my efforts failed did I sacrifice a sixpence and take legal possession. Through these opera glasses I then proceeded to leer with twelve-year-old lechery at the female dancers on stage. But then some male dancer entered my field of vision . . . I nearly fell off my seat. Eyes boggling, in tones of some considerable awe, I whispered, 'Cor! Look at 'is cobblers!'

And that, I regret to say, is virtually the only memory I have of my first visit to the ballet.

Years later, when I had left school and was at college in London, doing a drama course, I found to my initial unease that, as well as acting, we also had to dance – and that for Shakespeare we even had to wear tights! But, by now, my attitude towards such matters had matured, and during my drama-school training actually underwent a radical change. Appreciation took the place of bigotry, understanding of ignorance – although, being built like the proverbial brick wall, I never did quite manage to master the art of dancing.

I should like to think that society has grown far more tolerant than it was in my prejudiced youth, but I suspect that even today, while the idea of a working-class boy becoming an actor might not be thought of as suspect, if he expressed an interest in becoming a ballet dancer he might still have to contend with the Baboons and Roy Canaries of this world.

Jean Ure's very amusing novel *A Proper Little Nooryeff* took this situation and explored it with humour and zest. My aim in translating the book to the stage has been to present a play which, above all else, will be fun to perform, but which also raises issues which may invite discussion and hopefully cause any Baboons and Canaries who are out there to re-examine their prejudices. Why should anyone be frustrated in pursuing an objective simply because of the ignorance and stupidity of those around them?

Leonard Gregory

CHARACTERS
Students

JAMIE	15, straightforward and well-meaning, would rather please than not. Enjoys sport rather than more academic subjects.
ANITA	15, single-minded to the point of obsession; sometimes lacking in a sense of humour and awareness of others.
DOUG	15, easygoing and laid-back; prefers sex to school work. Loyal to his best mate, Jamie.
SHARON	15, very conscious of her own attractions; self-opinionated and likes to have her own way.
CORAL	15, Sharon's best friend; tends to live in her shadow.
KIM	10, Jamie's sister; uncomplicated and happy. Thinks the world of her brother but refuses to be squashed by him.
BOB PEARSON	17, an arrogant youth, accustomed to wielding power; aware of his appeal to the opposite sex.
ROY CANARY and THE BABOON	both 15, a couple of self-styled Jack-the-lads. Not a lot going for them.
DAVID	17, ambitious, personable, an easy mixer; a slight tendency to be theatrical.
GARSTIN	16, frets over minor details; not really a physical type and basically out of place in a theatrical setting – but was lured by the thought of girls.
ANDREA	10, Kim's mate at ballet class.
VARIOUS DEWDROPS	

Adults

MISS TUCKER	ballet teacher; an old-fashioned theatrical, elderly and set in her ways. Autocratic but not unsympathetic.

MR HUBBARD	maths teacher; could be any age. Egotistical, enjoys playing to an audience, can be sarcastic.
MR CARR	Jamie's Dad; a father of the old school. Conservative – with a small *c* – in his outlook but not a bigot.
MRS CARR	Jamie's Mum; a cheerful optimist, anxious that her kids should be happy and do well.
PIANIST	
WARDROBE LADY	

STAGE DIRECTIONS

There are two kinds of directions in this playscript. Those in **bold type** provide information that is essential to an understanding of what is happening in the play at the time. For a play-reading, these should be read by a separate reader.
Those in *italic type* are less essential stage directions and offer suggestions to assist with a production of the play on-stage. In a reading they are best not read out as they will hamper the flow of the play, although those who are reading may find that some of these instructions offer help with the interpretation of their lines.

SCENE 1

Miss Tucker's rehearsal room. A Friday evening during the summer term.

As the curtain rises we hear the rehearsal room piano, accompanied by the clop-thud of the DEWDROPS, amongst whom is KIM. MISS TUCKER and ANITA stand by the piano watching, ANITA in practice clothes. After a moment, the door opens and JAMIE puts his head round. Obviously rather embarrassed and feeling out of place, he sidles to a chair and sits down.

ANITA looks at JAMIE and says something to MISS TUCKER, who also looks. JAMIE becomes aware that they are discussing him. He grows uncomfortable. Finally, his nerve gives way, he gets up and heads back for the door.

MISS TUCKER nods in JAMIE'S direction, and ANITA at once glides after him. She detains him with a hand on his arm, forcing him to stand watching as the Dewdrop routine clops to a close.

MISS TUCKER All right, everyone, that was better than last time, but do try to remember that we are meant to be Dewdrops. Not cart horses. Kim, dear, watch those fingers. They look like bunches of twigs. Deirdre, remind me I want to look at your ankles some time. Andrea . . . yes. (*Looking sternly at Andrea*) I shall have a word with you tomorrow. Right! Off you go, then. Ten o'clock sharp in the morning. We'll take it straight through to Anita's solo. (*indicating Anita*)

(*The DEWDROPS curtsey, bobbing up and down like corks on the sea.*)

DEWDROPS (*In chorus*) Thank you, Miss Tucker. Good night, Miss Tucker.

MISS TUCKER (*With a gracious wave of the hand*) Good night.

(*The DEWDROPS disperse. KIM waves to JAMIE.*)

KIM Won't be long, Jamie!

(*ANITA follows the DEWDROPS out. JAMIE attempts to go with her but is stopped by MISS TUCKER.*)

MISS TUCKER	Young man! A word! You are Kim's brother, are you not?
JAMIE	Yeah. I came to pick her up.
MISS TUCKER	Yes, yes, yes! I am aware of that. Tell me! Are you musical?
JAMIE	Me?
MISS TUCKER	I am not in the habit of addressing the elements. Yes, you! Are you or are you not?
JAMIE	Not specially.
MISS TUCKER	You don't play anything?
JAMIE	Kim does. She c . . .
MISS TUCKER	(*Cutting in*) What about your sense of rhythm? Do you have a sense of rhythm? (*Pause.*) Can you move in time to music? If you hear a piece of music – Marjorie, dear! Could you give him something to move to?

(**The PIANIST strikes up an old-fashioned waltz.**)

There you are. Let's see what you can do.

(**JAMIE does nothing.**)

Well, go along! Do something!

JAMIE	Do what?
MISS TUCKER	Anything! Whatever you feel inspired to do.

(**Awkwardly, JAMIE shuffles a few paces forward.**)

Is that it? Come along, come along, young man! You can do better than that! Listen to the music. What is it telling you? It's telling you to *move*, is it not? Well, then . . . move! Let's see some action! *Yum* pum pum, *yum* pum pum . . . put some effort into it! Lift those feet! Shake out those shoulders! Good gracious me, anyone would think you were suffering from sleeping sickness! You don't have anything wrong with you, do you? If this is the way you carry on when you go to a disco . . .

JAMIE	(*goaded*) It's not the way I carry on when I go to discos! It's different at discos.
MISS TUCKER	How is it different?
JAMIE	Well, for one thing you're usually with a b . . . with a partner.
MISS TUCKER	Oh! Is that all that's stopping you? Well, that's easily remedied. Let's get with it!
	(MISS TUCKER seizes JAMIE by the hand and whirls him into the centre of the room. *(NB It is not important what Jamie and Miss Tucker dance. What is important is that Jamie should end up obviously enjoying it – and obviously being good at it.)* The piano stops.)
MISS TUCKER	Well! That was something different. I really quite enjoyed it!
	(The door opens and ANITA enters. She has changed out of her practice clothes. She crosses to MISS TUCKER.)
ANITA	Have you asked him?
MISS TUCKER	Do you know, I really think he'll do!
	(JAMIE looks from one to the other. MISS TUCKER takes him by the arm.)
MISS TUCKER	Come over here and stand by Anita.
	(She ranges him by Anita's side, measuring him with her eyes.)
	Yes! The match is perfect. Heightwise he couldn't be better . . . and I must say, he is excellently proportioned.
	(ANITA steps aside and also measures JAMIE with her eyes.)
MISS TUCKER	Do you do a lot of athletics?
JAMIE	Well, yeah, I suppose . . . quite a bit.
MISS TUCKER	I thought you must do. (*She squeezes his upper arm.*) That's why your muscles are so well developed. (*Pause.*) Well, now! How would you feel about helping us out?
ANITA	We're getting absolutely desperate. The show's going on in a few weeks' time.

MISS TUCKER   What we need is a Man.

JAMIE   What for?

ANITA   Just to *be* there. You wouldn't have to do much.

MISS TUCKER   Our only really mature young man, unfortunately, broke his arm last week in a motor cycle accident. I warned him time and again, such machines are lethal, but of course he wouldn't listen. Now he's in a plaster cast and quite useless.

ANITA   All we're left with are kids. And of course Garstin.

MISS TUCKER   Poor Garstin. He does try. But I'm afraid no amount of trying will compensate for lack of technique.

ANITA   Not to mention being able to keep time to the music.

MISS TUCKER   Oh, Kim's brother has an excellent sense of timing! He is naturally rhythmical. I have already made sure of *that*.

JAMIE   Look, what exactly . . .

ANITA   If I had to dance with Garstin, I'd rather not dance at all.

JAMIE   *Dance?*

MISS TUCKER   It's not as if we should want you here every night. Only just now and again, and occasionally for a private session with Anita.

(JAMIE looks at ANITA: he finds her attractive.)

You needn't worry that we'd ask you to do anything complex. There are only a couple of small lifts involved. I'm sure you wouldn't have any difficulty with those. I'm sure you could lift Anita with no trouble at all.

ANITA   And after all, it is for a good cause.

MISS TUCKER   Oh, yes. We always support a Cause. Last year it was Save the Children. This year it's Spastics. (*Pause.*) Didn't Kim say you had a little cousin who was spastic?

(JAMIE mumbles unintelligibly.)

	What? Speak up, young man, and don't swallow your words!
JAMIE	I said yeah . . . she goes to Fairfield.
ANITA	Fairfield!
MISS TUCKER	There you are! The very institution to whom we are giving the proceeds!
ANITA	It means we could put the Russian Dance back in! (*Spinning round to Jamie*) You could do a Russian Dance, couldn't you? Like the Red Army.

(ANITA demonstrates, down on her haunches with arms folded across her chest, legs kicking out. JAMIE watches.)

JAMIE	Yeah, well. I reckon I ought to be going now. My sister'll be waiting for me.
ANITA	But you will do it for us, won't you? (*A long pause.*) Please!
MISS TUCKER	We really should be most grateful. (*Another pause.*) And it is, after all, for Fairfield.
JAMIE	Yeah, I know, but . . . I'm not really into this sort of thing.
MISS TUCKER	There's always a first time.
JAMIE	Yeah, but . . .

(MISS TUCKER and ANITA wait for his answer.)

I dunno if I'd be any good.

MISS TUCKER	How can you tell until you've tried? Why not give it a go and see how it works out?
JAMIE	Well . . . (*Pause.*)

(JAMIE looks at ANITA.)

Oh, all right. I'll give it a go.

MISS TUCKER	Splendid!

ANITA Oh, Jamie, thank you! Maybe we could even put David's solo back in? Jamie could do David's solo!

JAMIE Hang about!

ANITA (*Cutting across*) It's not as if there's anything really technical – only right at the end.

MISS TUCKER Mmm . . . possibly. If we were to scale it down. We'll certainly think about it. Anyway! We'll see you at the next rehearsal, then, young man. I must remember to look you out some tights; you can't possibly dance in those things.

JAMIE Tights?

MISS TUCKER So much more comfortable than jeans. Look at you – you can't even bend your legs properly!

JAMIE I can!

MISS TUCKER Rubbish! Of course you can't.

JAMIE I can!

MISS TUCKER My dear boy, I have been in this business for forty years. I have taught household names. I know what I am talking about. What is your objection to wearing tights? Is there something wrong with your legs? Or are you simply prejudiced?

(MISS TUCKER looks at JAMIE. Jamie drops his gaze.)

MISS TUCKER Simply prejudiced! You disappoint me. I thought modern youth had grown out of that sort of thing. I thought you were more liberated. I see I was wrong. You are obviously still at the stage of infantile sniggering.

(ANITA starts to giggle and hastily smothers it.)

Let us have no more nonsense! No one can dance in skin-tight jeans. I shall look you out a pair of tights and you will wear them.

(Blackout.)

SCENE 2

The classroom. Mr Hubbard's maths class. The following Thursday afternoon. The lights fade up to reveal MR HUBBARD drawing geometric figures on the board while the CLASS watch, in various states of uninterest. There is a certain amount of chit-chat and horseplay. After a few seconds . . .

MR HUBBARD (*Back to the class, continuing to draw*) It will be interesting to see just how many of you budding geniuses will recognise any of these devices. Judging by the amount of noise, my efforts are not going unappreciated. At any rate they seem to be stimulating a certain degree of excitement . . . it gives me cause to hope that the level of ignorance I encountered last time we met might be a thing of the past. Like Micawber, I have great expectations.

(During the above, JAMIE is scribbling a note, shielding it with his hand to prevent DOUG from peering at it. DOUG is sitting beside JAMIE making a half-hearted attempt to see what he is writing and at the same time fumbling with one hand inside his desk. ROY CANARY is exchanging witticisms with the BABOON. SHARON is sitting at the front of the class pretending to be interested, her friend CORAL beside her. ANITA is at the back of the class, locked in a world of her own.)

MR HUBBARD (*Putting the finishing touches to one of his figures*) Well, now! Anyone care to hazard a guess as to what this figure represents?

(Silence. MR HUBBARD turns, briefly, from the board.)

No? Come along, come along! There must be intelligent life out there somewhere.

(More silence. All activity has ceased. MR HUBBARD scans the faces looking for some encouragement.)

Be a teacher, they said. It's so worthwhile, you'll find it so interesting. So stimulating. (*Abruptly, tiring of the game*) Right! Pay attention! (*He turns back to the board.*) Given that this is a right-angled triangle and that angle A equals 65°, does anyone have any ideas as to the size of angle C . . .?

(During the above, the sound of a transistor radio belting out pop music can be heard growing more intrusive by the second, together with loud uncouth voices, shouting. MR HUBBARD does his best to rise about it, while under cover of the noise DOUG whips his hand out of his desk and stuffs something into his mouth, JAMIE rips a page out of his exercise book, folds it and shoves it at DOUG. JAMIE indicates that the note is for SHARON. DOUG picks up his ruler and batters at a girl across the aisle, a couple of seats behind SHARON. He passes the note to her, nodding at SHARON, still concentrating on the board. MR HUBBARD suddenly throws down his chalk and strides to the door. He disappears into the corridor.)

MR HUBBARD (*Shouting, offstage*) Go and annoy somebody else, you cretins . . . and take that contraption with you!

(The music stops. DOUG turns to catch the eye of BABOON and CANARY. The note continues on its way to SHARON.)

DOUG I think Jimbo's in love . . .

(DOUG makes a lewd gesture. BABOON and CANARY fall about. JAMIE gives DOUG a shove which pushes him off his chair on to the floor, as MR HUBBARD reappears.)

JAMIE Piss off, ratbag!

(DOUG scrambles back on to his chair. Silence falls.)

MR HUBBARD (*Surveying the scene*) I trust you're sitting comfortably, Douglas? Feel quite free to express yourself, lad! No need to be bashful. If you've something to say, stand up and say it. Take the weight off your brain. Let us all have the benefit.

(As JAMIE gets to his feet we see SHARON opening the note.)

Well? Do you have something to say? (*Pause.*) You do not have something to say. Strange, I could have sworn I saw your lips move. Perchance you were but practising the art of silent ventriloquy?

(BABOON and CANARY like this: so does MR HUBBARD. He appreciates an audience.)

If that is the case, then I would strongly advise you in future to stick to one of the lesser known foreign languages. Preferably Serbo-Croat. Not everyone is as robust as your friend Douglas. Now, I wonder, if it's not putting you to too much trouble, whether I might tempt you to direct your attention to the angle marked C in the far corner of the figure marked 'one' upon the chalk board and be so good as to advise us as to its probable size?

(JAMIE has not the least idea as to the size of the angle. He is doing his best to keep an eye on SHARON.)

You have one in a hundred and eighty chances. That's a great deal better than the football pools.

DOUG Football pools are a load of crap.

CORAL That's all what you know. My dad won fifty quid on them last year.

DOUG Mug's game, innit.

MR HUBBARD Yes, and it's a mug's game not paying attention during my geometry lessons! Do you wish to grow up totally moronic? Because if so, you're going the right way about it.

(JAMIE says nothing. A pause. SHARON opens the note.)

Come on, Dozy! (*He flings chalk at Jamie.*) Look alive!

(Mechanically, JAMIE's hand shoots out and catches the chalk. Cheers, cries of 'Owzatt?', feet stamping etc. MR HUBBARD thumps his table.)

All right, settle down! I'm still waiting for the Professor here to set his powerful intellect in motion and release us from this terrible suspense . . . angle C, Professor! Enlighten us, if you please.

JAMIE 45°?

MR HUBBARD	Wrong!

(There is laughter, in which MR HUBBARD revels. SHARON titters; and aware that JAMIE is watching her, she drops the note to the floor without so much as a glance in his direction. JAMIE watches.)

Tell me, laddie, is it that you're bone idle, or are you just naturally thick?

(JAMIE stands, the butt of MR HUBBARD's wit. A pause, then MR HUBBARD turns his attention to a new victim.)

Sit down, boy! You're making the place look untidy. Miss Cairncross, I wonder if we might prevail upon you to join our little band of scholars? Perhaps you would condescend to give us the benefit of your opinion? Kindly glance at the board, study my modest handiwork, and let your mind run rampant. Who knows, you might be able to furnish us with the answer we so eagerly await?

(The class turn to look at ANITA, who sits as dumb as JAMIE. Pause.)

Please don't bother to stand up, Miss Cairncross. I do apologise for disturbing your reverie.

(ANITA starts to stand, but is saved by the sound of the klaxon.)

Ah, the relief of Mafeking! Go on, get out, the lot of you . . . *quietly*!

(The class disperse, noisily. MR HUBBARD fights his way through the mêlée. JAMIE and DOUG hang back, keeping an eye on SHARON and CORAL, who are taking their time. ANITA is still there, dreamily tidying away her books. SHARON and CORAL make for the door.)

JAMIE	Hey! Sharon!

(SHARON turns.)

What about my note?

SHARON	What about it?

JAMIE	I thought we were supposed to have a date tomorrow?
SHARON	Oh?
JAMIE	I already told Doug we'd see him down the disco (*Turning to Doug for confirmation*), didn't I?
DOUG	That's right.
SHARON	Did you?
JAMIE	Yes, I bloody did!
SHARON	Don't swear. I told you before. And don't shout.
JAMIE	(*Shouting*) Look. (*He controls himself.*) Look, when you tell someone you'll do something, you can't just back out at the last minute.
DOUG	That's right.
SHARON	Who's backing out? I don't remember being consulted. Seems to me some people take things a bit too much for granted. You've got a nerve – specially after last Friday.
JAMIE	I told you, it wasn't my fault. I got held up.
SHARON	That's what you always say.
JAMIE	Yeah, well, they don't always finish on time. I can't help it if they don't finish on time, can I?
SHARON	What d'you have to keep going and picking her up for anyway? Got two legs, hasn't she? Why can't she get home on her own like anyone else?
JAMIE	You know why! I told you – she has to go over the Common.
SHARON	So?
JAMIE	So it's not safe, a kid of that age.
DOUG	Nasty rough yobs over the Common.
SHARON	Who asked you, Megabrain? (*To Jamie*) What's she want to do ballet for, anyway? Stupid thing to do.

CORAL　Not as if she's ever going to get anywhere. You have to be slim, for ballet.

SHARON　Yeah, whoever heard of a dancing pumpkin? I'm sick of being messed about by you, James Carr . . .

(She turns to go, her arm through Coral's.)

(*Over her shoulder as they exit*) I should stick to child-minding, if I was you . . . you obviously can't handle women!

(SHARON and CORAL sweep out of the classroom.)

DOUG　Ah, well! Easy come, easy go. Personally I'd say you were better off without it – slag bag! (*To Jamie*) Cheer up! There's plenty more fish in the sea.

(ANITA has left her desk and is moving towards the door. DOUG and JAMIE are blocking her path.)

ANITA　Excuse me.

DOUG　Stand aside, James, and let the lady pass.

(JAMIE steps aside, as ANITA passes between.)

Now that is what I call quality (*as he and Jamie move to follow*). There was an old man from Calcutta, Who peeped through a hole in a shutter . . .

JAMIE　Belt up!

DOUG　All he could see. Was an old woman's knee . . .

(Blackout as JAMIE gives DOUG a shove through the door.)

SCENE 3

Miss Tucker's rehearsal room. The room is empty. After a few seconds JAMIE slinks in wearing the hated tights. He sidles up to a mirror and looks at himself. (*NB The actor playing Jamie can make as much or as little of this moment as the director feels is necessary.*) **Jamie starts as ANITA enters.**

ANITA　Oh, good! You're here.

(ANITA *starts limbering up at the barre.*)

Did you do that stuff for Miss Saville?

JAMIE   What stuff?

ANITA   That stuff on the War Poets.

JAMIE   Oh. Yeah. I done that.

ANITA   I couldn't find anything to say. Could you? I mean, I just couldn't think of anything. How much did you write?

JAMIE   Dunno. Couple of pages.

ANITA   (*Stopping to look at him*) Couple of *pages*?

JAMIE   Yeah, well . . . I got this big writing.

ANITA   Wish I had.

(ANITA *goes back to her exercises.* JAMIE *stands mute.*)

Miss Tucker'll be here in a minute.

(JAMIE *says nothing.*)

Don't you think you ought to start warming up?

JAMIE   I feel a right pillock.

ANITA   What? (*She stops.*) Why?

JAMIE   This lot.

ANITA   Tights?

JAMIE   I feel a right idiot.

ANITA   It's only a question of getting used to them . . . arctic explorers wear tights. Did you know?

(JAMIE *looks at her.*)

Honest! It's true. My uncle told me. He said there's nothing to beat a pair of tights for keeping the cold out . . . and he ought to know – he's been up Everest in them.

JAMIE   I've got an uncle like that . . . goes in for ladies' stockings.

ANITA   Ladies' stockings?

JAMIE   Yeah . . . wears 'em over his head every time he does a bank job.

ANITA   Are you serious?

JAMIE   What do you think?

ANITA   Well, I am! Men do wear tights. Anyway, I shouldn't worry too much . . . no one's going to be able to see anything – you'll have a nice long tunic to go over the top. Oh, come on! You promised.

JAMIE   I never promised to wear tights.

ANITA   You promised to dance – and you can't dance in jeans.

JAMIE   John Travolta does.

ANITA   That's a different sort of dancing.

JAMIE   Yeah. That's real dancing.

ANITA   You're just trying to get out of it!

JAMIE   I'm not trying to get out of it. But if I'm poncing about in this lot, you've got to promise me . . .

ANITA   What?

JAMIE   You've got to promise you won't tell anyone . . . specially not anyone at school.

ANITA   Oh, is that all? Of course I won't!

JAMIE   I mean it. You breathe so much as one word . . .

ANITA   I won't! I promise! Let's try the Russian Dance.

(ANITA goes down on her haunches, arms folded, and begins kicking out her legs. After a moment's hesitation, JAMIE can't resist it and joins in. After a few seconds MISS TUCKER enters. JAMIE freezes and slowly rises to a standing position.)

SCENE 3 15

MISS TUCKER Don't let me stop you, young man! That was looking very good. I told you you'd find tights a great improvement, didn't I? You'll find I do know what I'm talking about.

(MISS TUCKER is about to move across to the piano when KIM rushes in.)

KIM Miss Tucker, Miss Tucker! Can . . .

MISS TUCKER Not just now, Kim. I'll talk to you later, dear. We have work to do.

(As KIM turns to go, she sees JAMIE and rushes over to him.)

KIM You look great! Like a real dancer!

(JAMIE takes her by the arm and hustles her to the door.)

JAMIE Listen, you! I don't want a word of this getting out, right?

KIM But Jamie, why? You do, you look . . .

JAMIE (*Cutting across*) Just button it, OK?

KIM Can't I even tell Jacky?

JAMIE You tell anyone and I'll punch seven kinds of shit out of you.

(KIM turns away, then turns back.)

KIM What about Mum and Dad?

JAMIE I said *any*one.

(KIM looks at him for a second then exits.)

MISS TUCKER All right, young man! Are we ready to begin? (*To the pianist*) Marjorie, if you would be so kind?

(As the PIANIST strikes up, lights fade.)

SCENE 4

School corridor. Lights come up to reveal an empty corridor. A notice board is prominently displayed.
After a few seconds we hear the klaxon for end of class and the usual eruption of noise and confusion spills into the corridor. As the initial rush subsides we see DOUG and JAMIE, in cricket whites, DOUG with a ball. They wander up to the notice board to inspect the notices.

DOUG Hey, Jimbo, get a load of that! We made it! We made the team!

(JAMIE looks and gives a victory screech. Both boys leap up and punch the air.)

DOUG
JAMIE (*Together*) We are the greatest! We are the greatest!

(In the midst of their jubilation, SHARON and CORAL arrive. The boys almost bump into them.)

SHARON Do you mind?

CORAL You might look where you're going!

DOUG (*At the girls, shouting*) We are the greatest!

JAMIE We've made the first eleven!

SHARON Oh, big deal, big wheel!

CORAL Honestly, you'd think it was something important.

JAMIE It is important!

DOUG We're talking about the only thing that matters, lady!

CORAL Like a couple of kids.

SHARON In case you hadn't noticed, cricket is only a game.

DOUG That just goes to show what you know, dunnit?

(During the above, there have been various comings and goings of staff and pupils. SHARON is about to burst Doug's bubble when she spies the handsome BOB PEARSON strutting in their direction, dressed in his cricket whites, bat over his shoulder. JAMIE notices her gaze has transferred itself and turns to see what she is looking at.)

BOB (*To Jamie and Doug as he approaches*) You've seen the notice, I take it? You'd better come up with the goods, that's all I can say, because you won't be getting a second chance.

DOUG (*Saluting*) Jawohl, Herr General!

(SHARON is gazing at BOB, who so far has not taken any notice of her.)

BOB All I'm saying is that you've pestered me for a place on the team long enough. Well, now you've got the chance. Let's see if you can put the action where your mouth is.

SHARON (*Cutting in*) Hi, Rob!

BOB (*Catching sight of her*) Oh, hi, Sharon. How's it going?

SHARON Fine, thanks.

BOB Good!

(BOB struts off, watched by SHARON and CORAL.)

JAMIE What's with all this 'Hi, Rob' stuff?

SHARON What's it to you?

CORAL Yeah, what's it to you?

JAMIE (*Ignoring Coral*) Bob Pearson? He wouldn't look twice in your direction.

CORAL Oh, no?

(SHARON and CORAL link arms, as they push through the boys and march off.)

JAMIE You're not going out with him, are you?

SHARON Might be. Might not.

CORAL Might be. Might not.

(SHARON and CORAL exit. DOUG juggles with the ball.)

DOUG Like I said, there's plenty more fish in the sea. Anyway, we made the team.

JAMIE Yeah, that's right. We did!

(The two boys take up their refrain once more.)

JAMIE
DOUG (*Together*) We are the greatest! We are the greatest!

(Several members of Jamie and Doug's class have now entered the corridor, including CANARY and BABOON, with ANITA a little way behind. DOUG, with an exultant war cry, suddenly slings the ball at JAMIE.)

ANITA (*Screaming*) Jamie! Your hands!

(Whether JAMIE catches the ball or not, a sudden hush descends upon the corridor. The BABOON and ROY CANARY break the moment. They dance round JAMIE.)

BABOON
CANARY (*Together*) Oh, Jamie, your hands! Your ickle puddy paws? Watch the handy-wandies!

(BABOON and CANARY dance off, still singing.)

DOUG Yeah, well, I'd better be going. See you, Jimbo!

(DOUG exits, leaving JAMIE to confront ANITA. By now the corridor has cleared and they are alone.)

JAMIE What was that for?

ANITA Your hands! That was a hard ball! You could have damaged them!

JAMIE So what?

ANITA So you've got to dance. You've got to partner me!

JAMIE So nothing! I don't *have* to dance with anyone.

ANITA But you said. You promised! You can't back out now!

JAMIE Who says I can't?

ANITA Look, I'm sorry, I didn't mean to embarrass you. I was just worried in case you hurt yourself.

JAMIE	You were just worried in case I couldn't partner you.
ANITA	Well, of course I was! This is important!
JAMIE	So's cricket. A sight more important than some lousy ballet show.
ANITA	It's not a lousy ballet show! It's for Fairfield!

(JAMIE, stubborn, says nothing.)

Surely it wouldn't hurt you to just stop playing for a short while? Just until the show's over?

JAMIE	That wasn't any part of the deal!
ANITA	You never said then that you were playing cricket.
JAMIE	No, 'cause you never asked.

(A pause. They look at each other.)

ANITA	You're as bad as David. Miss Tucker told him it was dangerous, riding that bike.
JAMIE	Yeah? (*Tosses the cricket ball in the air*) So maybe some of us like living dangerously . . .

(JAMIE exits, leaving ANITA staring after him.)

SCENE 5

The CARRS' dining room, one Saturday morning. MR CARR, JAMIE and KIM are seated at the table eating toast and marmalade. MRS CARR is carrying cereal bowls out to the kitchen.

MR CARR	(*To Jamie*) You coming down the road with me tomorrow, then?
JAMIE	Down the road? What for?
MR CARR	One-day match, son!
JAMIE	Oh.
KIM	He can't tomorrow, we've got a rehearsal!

MR CARR   Now, come on, young lady. Fair's fair! You can get home under your own steam on a Sunday morning. Don't need your big brother to play escort all the time.

KIM   But he's in it!

MR CARR   In it? In what?

KIM   In the rehearsal . . . In the *show*.

MR CARR   What, him? Doing what? Molesting Dewdrops? (*Calling towards the kitchen*) Hear that, Pat? Your son's interfering with Dewdrops!

(JAMIE kicks out at KIM beneath the table. KIM, not taking the hint, carries on.)

KIM   He's not! Jamie's *dancing*. (*Pause*.) He's partnering Anita Cairncross.

MR CARR   Oh! Is he, indeed? Well well! Lucky old Anita Cairncross! Let's hope she enjoys it. Can't say that I would . . . clumsy great oaf like that.

KIM   Jamie's not clumsy. Miss Tucker says he's the most promising boy she's ever had. (*Jamie chokes on his toast*.) She does, Jamie.

(She reaches out for a piece of toast and begins smearing butter on it, several inches deep.)

Honest. I heard her talking to Anita. She said, he's the most promising boy I've ever had. And then she said something about, if we could only manage to convince him that it's . . . and then I couldn't hear any more because they walked away. Pass the honey.

JAMIE   Please.

KIM   Please. (*To Mr Carr*) Jamie and Anita are doing a *pas de deux*.

MR CARR   Oh, yes? And what's that when it's at home? Father of twins?

KIM   It's when two people dance together. With lifts, and things.

MR CARR   Lifts? You mean the sort that go up and down? First floor, second floor . . .

KIM   That's in buildings. Lifts in ballet are something different. It's where the man has to pick the girl up and carry her.

MR CARR   Ah, well, now you're starting to make sense! Picks her up and carries her, does he?

KIM   Yes, and then he has to support her when she does pirouettes and things. (*She jumps up.*) Come and show him, Jamie! I'll be Anita.

JAMIE   Why don't you just sit down and finish feeding your face!

MR CARR   Never tell me we're going to see those great hairy legs of yours encased in a pair of tights? How gruesome! That'll be a sight for sore eyes and no mistake.

(KIM sits down again and resumes her toast.)

KIM   Everybody wears tights.

MR CARR   Everybody hasn't got great hairy legs.

KIM   Jamie hasn't got great hairy legs! Miss Tucker says . . .

(MRS CARR comes in from the kitchen to collect some more empties.)

MRS CARR   (*Cutting across Kim*) Who's Anita Cairncross? Is she the girl with the nice voice that rang you up the other day?

KIM   She's the one he's dancing with. She's the best dancer in the whole school. She's going to do it full time next year.

MRS CARR   She sounded nice. Not like that other one. That Sharon, or whatever her name was. I never cared for that one. Always thought she'd lead you into bad ways. This one sounded quite different. (*Jamie hands his mother his cup and plate.*) Pretty, is she?

JAMIE   (*Getting in before Kim*) Not particularly.

KIM	Jamie, she *is*.
JAMIE	No, she isn't. She's skinny as a rake.
KIM	She isn't skinny, she's slim.
JAMIE	Well, whatever she is, she hasn't got any sex appeal.
MR CARR	A likely tale! Wink wink, nudge nudge . . . All I can say is, I wish you the best of British. You must have the nerve of old Nick!
JAMIE	*Look!*

(Startled, they all look up.)

It's for charity, isn't it? It's for spastics – it's for Fairfield. What am I supposed to say? When they ask me? What do I say? Stuff spastics? Is that what you want me to say? Stuff Auntie Carol and stuff Linda and stuff Fairfield? Is it?

(There is a silence.)

MR CARR	No. Well. Obviously it isn't. We all have to do our bit, best way we can. Only glad you've got a social conscience. Better than vandalising football pitches. So! When is it happening, this great event? I take it we shall be allowed to come?
KIM	You've got to come. Everybody's got to.
MR CARR	Everybody's got to! Well, that settles it, then, doesn't it? Don't worry yourself, lad! We'll take it seriously!
JAMIE	I'm not worried. It's not my show. I'm only doing it to help out.
MRS CARR	Of course you are. You mustn't mind your Dad, he's only joking. We're both very pleased. I think it's lovely you've offered to help them, I'm really quite proud of you.
MR CARR	So am I! I'll tell you what, you've got more guts than I'd have had at your age. You wouldn't have caught me prancing about in a pair of tights. Not for love nor money.

KIM But you have to wear them. You can't do ballet without tights.

MR CARR Is that a fact? I dunno! In my day, all we wanted was to play football for England.

KIM Football's only a game! Ballet dancers have to work far harder than footballers.

MR CARR Get away with you! Knees bend and point your toes . . . load of old nannies! Call that hard work?

KIM You put one of your rotten footballers in one of Miss Tucker's classes and he wouldn't last five minutes!

MR CARR You're dead right he wouldn't! Be too busy running for his life.

MRS CARR Well, it takes all kinds. Wouldn't do if we were all the same, would it?

MR CARR You can say that again. Anyway (*standing up*) I've got to be getting off. I'll see you later.

MRS CARR Yes, and I've got the hoovering to do. (*To Kim and Jamie*) You two can finish clearing the table and do the washing-up for me for a change.

KIM Pig's bum!

MRS CARR Yes, and pig's bum to you, madam! I don't ask that much of you.

MR CARR What's the matter? Ballet dancers too namby pamby to do the washing-up? (*Mr and Mrs Carr exit.*)

JAMIE Listen, you little cow, I thought I told you not to tell anyone?

KIM They had to know some time. I don't see why it should be kept a secret. Miss Tucker really did talk to Anita about you. I wish she'd say those kind of things about me.

JAMIE No chance, porky! Anyway, I'm not sure I'm going to do the show now.

KIM But you've got to!

JAMIE No, I haven't. In any case, I might not be able to.

KIM But Jamie, you told Miss Tucker you would!

JAMIE Yeah, well, that was before I knew about getting into the team.

KIM You can't let people down just for some stupid game of cricket!

JAMIE I'm not screwing my chances for some poxy kids' show. No way!

KIM I think you're being really horrible!

JAMIE And I think there's too many people taking things for granted.

KIM No one's taking you for granted. Miss Tucker thinks you're ever so kind. She was really upset when David broke his arm; she thought the whole show would have to be cancelled.

JAMIE (*Getting up and collecting breakfast things*) Still might, 'cause if I've got a match on the same day I'm going to be playing cricket!

(Blackout.)

SCENE 6

Rehearsal room. A few days later. JAMIE, dressed in normal street gear, is sprawled in one of the chairs trying hard to avoid eye contact with ANITA, who stands facing him. ANITA is dressed for rehearsal in leotard and tights. They are waiting for MISS TUCKER.

ANITA What's the matter with you? Why haven't you got changed? (*Pause.*) Jamie, Miss Tucker's going to be here any minute. You know she doesn't like wasting time. We have come here to dance, you know!

JAMIE Is that all you ever think about? Dancing?

ANITA   No, of course it isn't! But just at this moment . . .

JAMIE   So what else do you think about?

ANITA   Lots of things. Loads of things!

JAMIE   Tell me some.

ANITA   Jamie, this is not the time!

JAMIE   Do you ever think about the bomb and people starving and what it's like not to have money?

ANITA   Yes . . . sometimes. But now is not the . . .

JAMIE   You mean like once a year, maybe? Or once in two years?

ANITA   Well, how often do you?

JAMIE   More than you, I bet. Do you know, I've never heard you talk about anything that wasn't ballet?

ANITA   It's not because I'm not interested in other things. It's just that if you want to be a dancer there simply isn't room for anything else. If you really want to get anywhere . . .

JAMIE   Crap!

ANITA   Jamie, it's not crap! It's true! Imagine if you wanted to be a footballer, or a cricketer, or a . . . a pop star, or something. Imagine how hard you'd have to work . . . all those training sessions – all the practice. Well, it's exactly the same with dancing. It's just no *use* thinking you can skip class every time you're feeling a bit off or something a bit more interesting turns up. You have to put ballet first.

JAMIE   Yeah – that's if you're going to be a dancer.

ANITA   I'm sure you could be, if you wanted. If you tried for ballet school . . .

JAMIE   Me? I'm not trying for any ballet school! My old man would have a fit.

ANITA Is that the only thing that stops you?

JAMIE No, it is not! If you want to know the truth, I don't reckon I ought to be doing this lot.

(There is a pause. ANITA looks at him.)

ANITA Why not?

(JAMIE gets up and moves moodily about the room. ANITA watches him.)

JAMIE I dunno. Just doesn't seem . . . right. I s'pose.

ANITA What do you mean, it doesn't seem right? What doesn't seem right?

JAMIE This dancing lark. My Dad . . . (*Anita waits.*) My dad reckons dancers are a load of old nannies.

ANITA Oh, well! Your Dad! It's the stupid sort of thing someone's Dad would say, isn't it? I bet *your Dad* doesn't know the first thing about it . . . I bet he couldn't tell an *entrechat* from an *arabesque*.

(JAMIE says nothing.)

I suppose it would be all right if you wanted to be a boxer. That's manly, isn't it? Two men knocking the life out of each other . . . that's really manly, that is.

(JAMIE maintains his silence.)

(*Trying another tack*) Warriors dance. Look at African tribes – look at Zulus. Look at Cossacks! What about the Red Army? It's always the men.

JAMIE It's different for them.

ANITA How? Dancing's dancing, isn't it? (*Pause.*) Miss Tucker said we'd have trouble. She said you'd think it was compromising your masculinity.

JAMIE I don't think it's compromising my masculinity.

ANITA All right, then! So if you're not scared that it's poufy and that people are going to laugh at you, why don't you want to do it? (*Pause.*) It's because you *are* scared that they're going to laugh at you! You are, and you just won't admit it! You're such a coward!

JAMIE No, I'm not.

ANITA Yes, you are! It bothers you, what other people think. *You* don't think it's poufy, but . . .

JAMIE How do you know? How do you know I don't?

ANITA Because if you did you wouldn't be any good at it. And you are good at it. Miss Tucker thinks you could really get somewhere if you were prepared to work.

JAMIE Yeah, well, I'm not. Not at dancing, at any rate . . . Please, sir! I'm going to ballet school . . . Doug would die laughing.

ANITA You mean you'd sooner spend your life doing some boring, soulless job in a factory than be a dancer?

JAMIE Who says I'm going to do some boring soulless job in a factory?

ANITA All right! So what are you going to do?

JAMIE I'm going to play cricket . . . and what's more, I'm going to play it on Saturday.

ANITA Saturday? But that's the day of the show!

JAMIE I know.

ANITA So how can you possibly play cricket?

JAMIE Look, I already told you. I am not stopping playing cricket for you or anyone else.

ANITA Jamie, I know you think I'm just being stupid and making a fuss, but I'm not. Honestly, I'm not! I'm really *not*. You've only got to sprain something, or pull a muscle, or even just bruise yourself . . .

JAMIE So what are you suggesting? I should wear a suit of armour?

ANITA Imagine if you got knocked out!

JAMIE Then you'd have to dance with Garstin, wouldn't you?

ANITA I wouldn't dance with Garstin if he were the last man left on earth! I wouldn't be seen dead on the same stage with Garstin!

JAMIE So that's your problem. I can't guarantee I'm not going to get knocked stone cold. It's a chance you'll have to take.

ANITA You mean you really are going to play?

JAMIE You'd better believe it. And as a matter of fact, I'm not even certain I'm going to be able to make the dress rehearsal on time. We've got a net practice that goes on till seven on Friday evening. I might just be able to get there for seven-thirty. On the other hand, I might not. (*There is a long pause.*)

ANITA You'd better tell Miss Tucker.

JAMIE Don't worry. I will.

(As JAMIE speaks, MISS TUCKER and the PIANIST enter. ANITA looks hard at JAMIE, who avoids her stare.)

MISS TUCKER Good evening, Anita, Jamie! I trust you're both well? Someone arrived late, I suspect, judging by the state of his dress . . . off with you! Out of those clothes! We've got a lot of work to get through.

(As ANITA waits for JAMIE to respond . . . Blackout.)

SCENE 7

School corridor. The following day. The usual hustle and bustle with kids and staff all going somewhere. BOB PEARSON enters, carrying a sheet of paper. He pins the paper on the notice board. The corridor begins to clear and we see JAMIE enter. BOB is just about to go when he notices JAMIE approaching.

BOB I've just made Saturday's team official. Don't forget – nets on Friday evening.

SCENE 7   29

JAMIE   Yeah. OK. Er . . . would it be . . . OK, er . . . all right if I . . . er . . . left at five-thirty?

BOB   No, it would not! You need all the practice you can get. Didn't you miss out on last week's?

JAMIE   That was a mistake. I wouldn't have done, if I'd known. I didn't know you wanted me.

BOB   So whose fault was that? You should have kept your eyes on the board as you're supposed to. You knew quick enough when you were selected for the team!

JAMIE   Yeah, I just can't get used to the five-minute updates.

BOB   Button it, smart arse! You either want to be in the team and are interested in what goes on, or you're not!

JAMIE   I am!

BOB   So what's with this sloping off early on Friday?

JAMIE   It's just that I promised somebody. Ages ago. I promised I'd do something.

BOB   Well, if it's some bird you were thinking of taking somewhere, you can forget it.

JAMIE   It isn't a bird.

BOB   So what is it, then?

JAMIE   (*Hesitating*) It's helping out with a show. For spastics.

BOB   On Friday evening?

JAMIE   Yeah . . . Well, that's when the dress rehearsal is. I told them I'd be there.

BOB   You told them you'd be there on a Friday evening? When you know perfectly bloody well that that's when net practices are held? Well, I'm sorry! I don't have people on the team with divided loyalties. To me, the team comes first. You either play cricket or you go off and do this other thing. It's up to you.

JAMIE   But it's for spastics!

BOB   I don't give a toss what it's for! It could be for snow-blind huskies, for all I care. I've got a job to do, getting a team together. I need people who can be relied on. Like I said, you either want to be a part of the action or you don't. If you do, you'll turn up on Friday and stay till seven the same as everyone else. If you don't, you'd better tell me now so I can make alternative arrangements. The decision is yours. (*Long pause.*) Well, come on! I haven't got all day. Which is it to be? Us or Them?

JAMIE   I just don't like letting people down.

BOB   Which people?

JAMIE   Well . . . them.

BOB   I see. You don't mind letting the school down; that doesn't bother you.

JAMIE   It does! But . . . but they're spastics!

BOB   Well, unless you can perform a miracle and be in two places at the same time, someone's going to get the bum's rush!

(JAMIE *starts to say something.* BOB *cuts in.*)

People like you I can do without. (*He produces a felt tip pen.*) You needn't bother looking on the notice board in future, Carr; your name will certainly not be there any more – at least, not in connection with cricketing activities. Not while I'm captain!

(JAMIE *watches in stunned disbelief as* BOB *strikes out his name and, without further acknowledging* JAMIE, *strides off.*)

(*To no one in particular*) That takes care of that!

JAMIE   (*To Bob's receding back*) Fascist scum!

(DOUG *now appears from one direction as* SHARON *and* CORAL, *arm in arm, appear from the other.*)

DOUG   (*Approaching Jamie*) We must stop meeting like this, Jimbo! People will say we're in love.

SCENE 7   31

JAMIE   Bug off.

DOUG   Now, now! We'll have less of that sort of language. There are ladies present.

(SHARON and CORAL giggle as they join the two boys at the board.)

SHARON   Hi, Jamie!

(DOUG turns to look at the notice board.)

JAMIE   What d'you want?

CORAL   Charming!

SHARON   (*To Coral*) He's dead smooth. You've got to give him that.

JAMIE   So what d'you want?

SHARON   My friend and I would like to look at the notice board if there's no law against it.

(JAMIE steps to one side.)

SHARON   And I had thought of asking you to take me out on Friday but I'm very rapidly going off the idea.

JAMIE   Good! So just get off my back.

DOUG   (*Turning from the notice board*) What's with all this, Jimbo? (*Pointing at the team listing*) What's he scrubbed you out for?

JAMIE   Went off me.

DOUG   Why? What you been up to? (*Indicating Sharon*) It's not because of her, is it?

SHARON   Cheek! What makes you think I got anything to do with it?

JAMIE   It's nothing to do with her. It's between him and me. Don't worry about it.

DOUG   But I do, Jimbo! I do! Oh, come on, you can tell me – I am supposed to be your best mate! What you been up to?

CORAL Yeah, what you been up to, Jimbo?

(At this point our attention is distracted by the sudden arrival of CANARY and BABOON, who go squawking past the foursome at the board.)

BABOON (*Together*) Jamie, your hands! Poor ickle puddy-
CANARY wuddies . . .

SHARON (*Watching Baboon and Canary as they go*) What was all that about? What's the matter with your hands?

JAMIE Nothing. Just ignore them.

CORAL They're bananas, them two.

SHARON So, anyway. What about it?

JAMIE What about what?

SHARON Friday!

JAMIE Friday?

CORAL Comes after Thursday, Dumbo! Day after tomorrow, in case you hadn't noticed.

SHARON You going to take me to the disco or not?

JAMIE Oh! That. No . . . I can't. Got something else on. Sorry.

SHARON Right. That is the last time I'll do you any favours, Jamie Carr. You needn't try crawling round me in future.

(SHARON pulls CORAL after her, leaving the two boys at the notice board.)

CORAL (*Over her shoulder*) Get back in your dustbins, the pair of you! You're junk!

DOUG Yeah, and you're rubbish! (*To Jamie*) Pair of scrubbers! What's all this about you and Pearson?

JAMIE Look, I don't want to talk about it. OK? Just drop it.

DOUG I think you're trying to hide something, Jimbo – you've obviously upset him. What did you do? Catch him sniffing his jock strap, or what?

JAMIE   I said drop it, didn't I? I'm bored with the subject. Just get off my back and leave me alone!

DOUG   All right. If that's the way you feel about it, I'll nip over to the zoo and strike up a relationship with a porcupine. Should be quite pleasant after this.

(As DOUG turns to go he bumps into MR HUBBARD, who is on the point of pinning a notice of his own to the board.)

DOUG   Sorry, sir.

MR HUBBARD   Quite all right, Douglas. My, we are becoming civilised!

(DOUG exits. As MR HUBBARD leans in to pin his notice he catches sight of the cricket listing.)

MR HUBBARD   What's this? Changed your mind about playing cricket?

JAMIE   Looks that way, sir.

MR HUBBARD   (*Moving off*) Don't tell me, you're taking up mathematics instead!

(A bark of laughter from MR HUBBARD, amused by his own wit. Blackout.)

SCENE 8

Stage of church hall, pre-performance. As the lights come up, we see:
– assorted DEWDROPS galloping excitedly on and offstage, screaming and calling out to each other, and MISS TUCKER;
– MISS TUCKER talking to a tall good-looking boy with his arm in a sling, DAVID;
– JAMIE wandering on stage (in his tights) looking somewhat uneasy;
– KIM skipping up to him;
– ANITA appearing in her tutu, looking every inch the ballerina, and making a beeline for MISS TUCKER and DAVID;
– JAMIE watching (none too pleased) as DAVID plants a theatrical kiss on ANITA'S cheek;
– a long stringy beanpole, GARSTIN, coming on stage in blue tights, carrying a blue jerkin in one hand, and attempting to show it to various uninterested people, finally homing in on JAMIE.

GARSTIN (*Brandishing his garment at Jamie*) Look at this! They've used nylon thread all round the neck. I can't possibly wear it, it'll bring on my allergy. Who's doing wardrobe?

(The WARDROBE LADY detaches herself from a group of DEWDROPS.)

WARDROBE LADY What's the matter, Garstin?

GARSTIN I can't wear this, it's got nylon thread. I'm allergic to nylon. How can I go on as Little Boy Blue if I'm bright red?

WARDROBE LADY You might have thought of it a bit earlier! The doors'll be opening any second.

GARSTIN How was I to know? It says 100% cotton. It wasn't till I put it on . . .

WARDROBE LADY Come on, then, quickly! Let's see what we can do.

(The WARDROBE LADY moves to exit. GARSTIN follows, grumbling.)

GARSTIN It's always the same. You buy things that say they're cotton, then you find they've gone and stitched them up with nylon. I can't wear nylon. It brings me out in this rash . . .

(GARSTIN's voice fades as he exits. DAVID, meanwhile, has crossed to JAMIE.)

DAVID So you're the prodigy? I'm David. I've been hearing great and wonderful things about you.

JAMIE I got press-ganged. You want to take over again, you're quite welcome.

DAVID (*Indicating sling*) With this? Anyway, to be quite honest with you I'm not too sure what sort of a welcome I'd get. At any rate, I'd rather not have to put it to the test . . . from all accounts, my son, you're something of a budding genius . . . a proper little Nooryeff!* (*Slight pause.*) True as I stand here . . . Thea Tucker's been singing your praises. If your ears aren't burning, they ought to be. I tell you, she's gone ape . . . according to her, you're what's known as a natural. Don't need to be taught like the rest of us. Who's a lucky boy? They'll be doing a Russian spectacular next. Just to put you through your paces.

JAMIE There's not going to be any next. I'm only helping out just this once.

DAVID Don't you kid yourself! Once Thea gets her hands on a bit of talent, she doesn't let go that easily. She's already got a great future mapped out for you. Royal Ballet School, Royal Ballet . . .

JAMIE Leave it out.

DAVID You'd better believe it! What Thea wants, Thea gets. She got you, didn't she? Right where she wants you . . . anyway, I must be off and find my seat. Break a leg, Megastar!

JAMIE Yeah. Thanks.

(DAVID *crosses back to* MISS TUCKER. ANITA *moves over to be with* JAMIE.)

ANITA You all right?

JAMIE I s'pose so.

ANITA Cricket *is* only a game.

JAMIE Hmm!

(During the above exchanges the confusion on stage has continued. GARSTIN now reappears, wearing his top and scratching. DAVID exits. MISS TUCKER claps her hands for attention.)

---

* *Rudolph Nureyev.* Famous Russian ballet dancer, defected to the West in 1961.

MISS TUCKER Now, come on! Settle down, everybody! Let's clear the stage of all unwanted bits and pieces and get set-up for the first routine. Anybody not involved in doing anything useful, please leave the stage. Those in the opening sequence, check your costumes and take up your positions. And can we please try to do it quietly! People will be coming in at any moment. We don't want to frighten them away, do we?

DEWDROPS (*Variously*) No, Miss Tucker! Yes. Miss Tucker!

MISS TUCKER Jamie, you should be over there (*pointing to a spot in the wings*) opposite Anita. Garstin, do stop scratching! Dewdrops, get into your circle. Come along, now, come along!

(The DEWDROPS scurry off to form their circle. The stage is cleared of unwanted bits and pieces. All exit save for the DEWDROPS and MISS TUCKER. JAMIE and ANITA take up their positions in the wings, on opposite sides.)

MISS TUCKER We seem to have a Dewdrop missing! Who's missing?

(ANDREA scuttles on stage.)

Come along, Andrea! For goodness' sake! The performance is tonight, not tomorrow.

ANDREA Yes, Miss Tucker. Sorry, Miss Tucker.

(ANDREA dives into her place in the circle.)

MISS TUCKER Now, keep it quiet! We're putting the lights out, so be careful . . . and good luck, everybody!

DEWDROPS Thank you, Miss Tucker. Good luck, Miss Tucker.

(The lights go out. We can hear GARSTIN mumbling about his nylon thread and the DEWDROPS whispering and giggling. There is a loud thud as someone trips over something.)
(NB During the blackout MR and MRS CARR, and DAVID, join the audience.)

A VOICE Someone's fallen over.

MISS TUCKER	Be quiet!
	(There is silence.)
KIM	Miss Tucker, Andrea's feeling sick.
MISS TUCKER	*Quiet!*

(The piano starts, the lights fade up. Slowly (to the strains of 'Morning' from *Peer Gynt* perhaps) we see the DEWDROPS arise and go into their routine.)

(NB The nature and duration of the dance sequences which follow will obviously be governed by the individual circumstances of each production. The only essential, whether the dancing lasts five minutes or fifteen, is that the culmination should be JAMIE and ANITA dancing together. The following framework is only a suggestion.)

DEWDROPS
followed by
GARSTIN and TWO GIRLS
followed by
DEWDROPS
followed by
Solo for JAMIE (Russian Dance)
Solo for ANITA (Classical))
Pas de Deux (JAMIE and ANITA)

(During the *pas de deux*, BABOON and CANARY, who have crept in at the back of the hall, start barracking JAMIE.)

BABOON	Oh! What a tantalising twirl!
CANARY	*(Joining in)* Lovely pair o' calves you got there, darling!
BABOON	Let's see you do the splits!

(Various members of the audience – including MR and MRS CARR – make outraged shushing noises. JAMIE visibly reacts but carries on dancing. His enjoyment should be obvious in spite of the interruption.)

BABOON	Hey, Jamie, what about your hands?

CANARY   What a lovely little mover!

BABOON   Right little twinkletoes!

MR CARR   Belt up, you morons!

(Silence as JAMIE and ANITA dance.)

CANARY   Oh, what a gay day!

BABOON   Why don't you give her one?

(MR CARR, possibly aided by DAVID, gets up and collars the two offenders.)

MR CARR   Go on! Get out, the pair of you!

BABOON
CANARY   *(Together)* Hey, leggo! Gerroff! *(As they are ejected)*

BABOON
CANARY   *(Together)* We didn't mean nothing! We're into ballet!

(The door slams behind them. The dancing has continued during the above exchange and now reaches its climax . . . The FULL COMPANY returns to the stage for the final dance sequence. The lights go down. The DEWDROPS, GARSTIN, JAMIE and ANITA take their curtain calls.)

MR CARR   *(On his feet)* Bravo!

(The FULL COMPANY assembles, with JAMIE and ANITA centre stage. As the lights dim for last time Anita plants a big thank you kiss on JAMIE'S cheeks, leaving him gob-smacked . . .)

The End

WRITING THE PLAY

I have written plays before, but always using my own original ideas and material, which on balance I think was easier than adapting a book, because I was able to choose the shape and the conventions to be employed.

When it came to this particular play I was confronted by characters that were already formed, a situation that had already been worked out, and the knowledge that some of the students who might be reading or putting on the play would be familiar with the original book by Jean Ure. That is pretty daunting, believe me. I had visions of stroppy students informing their English teacher or Drama teacher that 'This is not in the book,' or (which is even worse) 'I don't like this as much as the book.'

Inevitably, there are minor differences, because what works in book form doesn't necessarily transfer directly to the stage. The biggest differences are in the chronology, or the order in which things happen. To give an example, just take our introduction to Jamie and Doug. In the book, we first meet them in the classroom, with Mr Hubbard; in the play, we first meet Jamie in the rehearsal room, along with Anita and Miss Tucker, while Doug doesn't appear until the next scene. Basically it happens this way because I would have had trouble in two respects – one, there would not have been sufficient time to create the story both convincingly and dramatically; and two, I would have had to have two rehearsal room scenes running one after the other. I could have stuck to the original chronology only by having more scenes and by inventing more dialogue, and this was a compromise I didn't wish to make, as it might have changed the whole feel of the original.

In fact, the only dialogue that I have created is for Bob Pearson, in his first scene. Apart from this, the rest is almost all Jean Ure, although in some cases – for instance, Garstin and his nylon thread – I have had to translate reported speech into direct speech. Occasionally, too, I have 'lifted' dialogue from one scene and incorporated it in another, since it has obviously not been possible to include all the scenes from the book. The most important thing, however, is not so much the preservation at all costs of original dialogue but the creation of a sense of fun, the excitement of doing and enjoying the actions of the book in a real, physical, here-and-now way, so that those who have not read the book will feel that they would like to.

Leonard Gregory

Ground-plan for scenes

Scenes 1, 3 and 6 *Rehearsal room*

Portable barre and mirrors would add authenticity, but scene can be done without.

Scene 2 *Classroom*

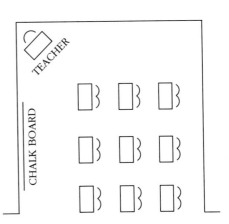

Scenes 4 and 7 *School corridor*

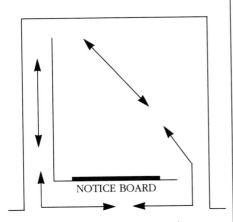

Corridor is indicated by the use of portable acoustic screens. Arrows show how staff and pupils can circulate.

Scene 5 *Carrs' dining room*

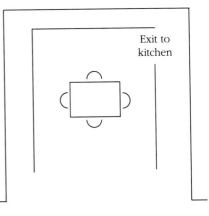

Dining room is enclosed within screens.

FOLLOW-UP ACTIVITIES

A Proper Little Nooryeff is a play which, through its story about a boy's introduction to dance, explores the problems of prejudice and stereotypes. We all use prejudices and stereotypes in our everyday thinking in order to make sense of the world. A prejudice is a *pre-judgement*; we attempt to understand a situation by referring back to our past experience and assuming that what we are seeing or hearing now shares some of the same features. The problem with this habit is that it then blinds us to what is different about the situation we have encountered. Jamie does this when he is first asked whether he will help out by performing in the dance show. He believes that men don't dance, despite the evidence offered by Miss Tucker, of all the different cultures where men are dancers. Of course, Jamie is partly right. Too few boys and men understand that ballet, or other forms of classical and modern dance, are suitable activities for males and so they do not get involved. Fortunately, there are boys and men who do not allow this prejudice to inhibit them and so we are privileged to have dancers such as Rudolph Nureyev, Wayne Sleep, Michael Clark and Darshen Bhuller.

Prejudice develops into a problem when we refuse to alter our beliefs despite having new and different evidence in front of us. Prejudice is a problem when it is used against other people and infringes their rights. At its extreme, of course, prejudice becomes bigotry. Roy Canary and The Baboon are clear examples of unintelligent bigots.

Discussion

- Try, as a group, to come up with definitions of
    - prejudice
    - stereotype
    - caricature
    - bigotry.

    In your discussion, you may like to consider whether any of these categories can have positive as well as negative features. Do the four words describe four quite different things, or do they spill into one another?

- Coral says that Jamie's sister, Kim, is unlikely to be successful as a ballet dancer because 'you have to be slim' and

Sharon adds, unkindly, '. . . whoever heard of a dancing pumpkin?'. Why does she say this and do you think it is true? You might like to start by listing what kinds of physique are necessary for the following activities:

    contemporary dance   soccer
    basketball   rugby
    swimming   weightlifting
        sprinting.

Can you now think of successful people who contradict the physique that you have suggested? One example is that many of these activities are undertaken by people who use wheelchairs for mobility – and they take the sport to Olympic standard.

- We are aware that fashion changes. Even over very small periods of time, items of clothes, haircuts and make-up can quickly pass in and out of favour. However, the same is true of bodies. A quick flick through fashion magazines over the last fifty years will show that different body types are fashionable for models at different times. This is just as true for men as it is for women. You may like to discuss the reasons for the use of corsets; padded shoulders in jackets for men and women; the appeal of lycra clothing; the fact that pale skins for white people were once considered beautiful and that now we tend to favour sun-tans (although the health problems associated with skin melanoma from over-exposure to the sun may change this).

Designing the play

Over recent years, many of our street fashions have borrowed ideas from sports and dance wear. The most obvious example is the use of lycra and the popularity of footless tights. Miss Tucker's dance school is a little old-fashioned. In designing the set and costumes for the play, this will have to be borne in mind. However, it is very easy to stereotype and you will need constantly to bear in mind ways that Miss Tucker can surprise us in her behaviour to suggest that she is not a caricature. After all, she does understand the pressures that Jamie feels to conform to a particular male model and skilfully changes

Jamie's mind and, along the way, the prejudices of a number of other people. The play uses humour – you can enhance this in the way you design the costumes and the set. Have fun putting together your production!

- The writer of the play, Leonard Gregory, has provided us with a series of very basic floor-plans. These are for a proscenium-arch stage where the audience watch the performance from the front, as if a wall had been removed from the action. This may not suit the sort of theatre space you will be using and your first task may be to work out new settings for a performance that will have the audience on three sides (a thrust stage) or on all four sides (in-the-round). Each style has its own problems and you will have to bear in mind the need for clear sightlines so that every person in the audience can see all the action all the time.

    Begin by sketching plans of your own theatre, studio or hall. Having done this, you can begin to go through the play and plot each scene, so that each space for the activity has its own set. Once you've done this, you might like to draw your plans to scale. This will involve taking measurements of the hall and deciding on the dimensions of the objects on your set.

    Having done this, prepare some sketches of the actual views of the set. What you have already done is provide floor-plans which give us a bird's-eye view of the set. The project now is to provide an impression of the view the audience will have.

    If you are very ambitious, you may like to build a three-dimensional model using stiff card or very light cardboard. This could either be in scale or simply an impression. The value of a model is that it becomes a very good guide for the builders of the set and helps the director with the job of moving actors around the acting space.

- It is very useful, from a very early stage in the rehearsals, to have as many props available as possible. The first task is to read the play very thoroughly and note down every item that is needed for the characters to fulfil their roles. For example, there will be books, pens, paper and chalk for the classroom, cricket balls and bats for other scenes, and the dance scenes may have their own needs. You may need items for dressing the set that aren't strictly necessary and you will need to use your imagination for this. For example, it may be useful to have a rosin box for the dance studio scenes. If you don't know what a rosin box is you'll need to go and speak to someone who is a dancer and while you're about it, find out what other things you're likely to find in a dance studio!

Once you have made your list, you will need to begin finding sources from which to borrow or, if necessary, buy the items. It's a very good idea to keep a small notebook in which to make a record of the item, where it came from and, if bought, how much it cost. There is nothing worse than ending up, after a production, with items to return to people and no memory of where they were borrowed from. It's also important to keep a tally on costs, so that you know that you are not exceeding the budget and that you will be reimbursed for any money that you do have to spend.

- There are a wide variety of characters to design and make costumes for. There are also some characters who will need costume changes, such as Anita and Jamie who will need everyday clothes, rehearsal tights and their performance outfits. You might like to begin by designing costumes for a limited number of characters. Bear in mind their personalities and how this may affect the way they dress.

  Begin by making brief notes on the characters and then draw sketches of what you think they might wear. For example, you may choose Mr Hubbard, the teacher. He is crusty and sarcastic and something of a stereotype of a certain kind of teacher. What do such teachers tend to wear?

  As you get into more detail, you will need to begin thinking about colour and materials. Some productions choose to limit the colours of costumes and set so that the whole production has an over-all theme. Are you going to do this? If you are, you will need to speak with the director and the set-designer beforehand. Where will the clothes come from? How many can you borrow? What will need to be bought? What will need to be made? Are there people with sewing skills to help? Make notes on all these points so that you know you have planned well.

Movement

The playwright makes the point that the dance sequences can be as simple or as ambitious as suits the ability of the dancers in the cast. It is often the case that a simple exercise done well is much more impressive for an audience than a complicated manoeuvre done badly. Whatever level of dance you choose, it will be important to rehearse the pieces well and spend time on the detail of the choreography. The play itself suggests that some of the dance sequences are less than perfectly performed. For instance, the Dewdrops have their movement described as a 'clop thud'. However, this is not to suggest that you put a group of unrehearsed dancers on your stage thinking that because the sequence will be done badly, through lack of practice or ability, it will look realistic. It will simply look terrible. To achieve the humour that is implied in the 'clop thud' will involve your dancers in doing the sequence as well as possible and *then* choreographing in the mistakes. There will be the one dancer who may be consistently out of time, another who turns the wrong way, another who wants to be noticed above all the other dancers, and yet another who is busy looking for her special friend in the audience.

The following are a number of choreography exercises that will be important for your production. Even if you have no dance or movement experience at all, the first two suggestions will be within your skill.

- There is a very simple piece of stage movement in Scene 2 on page 8, in which Jamie rips a page out of a book and passes it on as a note. Try choreographing this so that the audience's attention is drawn to the sequence of events but it still remains a devious activity that takes place behind the teacher's back. Aim for slickness and humour in the way it is worked out.

- In Scene 2 on page 9, Mr Hubbard throws a piece of chalk which Jamie thrusts up an arm to catch and calls 'Owzatt?'. Jamie's action is almost reflexive and his speed comes from being an able cricket player. The chalk should not appear to have been thrown purposefully at Jamie for the sequence to be really funny. It is apparently quite straightforward but you will have to plan and time this in some detail. It needs simplicity and precise timing in its execution. Work closely with your actors and plot what works best for them. Rehearse it as often as you can and watch closely to see if anything is going wrong in case catches are missed or whether there are ways of improving it so as to increase the comic intention.

- Choreograph the opening Dewdrop routine. If you are used to working with any form of dance notation, you might like to begin by jotting your ideas down on paper. If you don't have this ability, it isn't a problem. Work with your dance group and take the sequence phrase by phrase. Do not be tempted to work in the mistakes until the dancers have fully learnt the sequence and you have ironed out the problems. Then you can have fun with including the mistakes, although it's probably a good idea not to overdo it! Your dancers will have ideas, too, and it will be important to include their thinking and have yours changed along the way.

- Very early in the play (page 3), Jamie and Miss Tucker find themselves dancing together. For this piece of choreography you will need to work out the actual dance sequence and then pace the dance so that we, the audience, can see the change from resistance, on Jamie's part, through to enjoyment at the end. The dancers will also have the challenge of portraying different ages even if, in reality, they are the same age. How can this be achieved?

- The climax of the dance show is the *pas de deux* between Jamie and Anita. Choreograph this sequence remembering that it should be seen as being the high-point of the dance and the ability of the dancers need to be shown off. If the dancers are not trained to a high degree, remember to keep the movement very much within their range. One or two tricky moments successfully manoeuvred will work much better than an overly ambitious dance.

Project

How often have you heard people say that they have just seen a film that wasn't as good as the book? Or read the book and it wasn't as good as the film? You have probably said it yourself. It is a very difficult judgement to make because we wouldn't necessarily agree on what 'good' means; are we talking about the special effects, the use of language, the costume and sets, the story lines, the characterisation and the acting? What we often mean when we make such comments is that we had a very particular picture of the film, play or book and that another interpretation does not match our prejudices. If you read the section *Making the Play*, Leonard Gregory talks of the problems involved in turning the book into a drama script. He has tried very hard to stay as close to the book's format as possible.

If you were to make a film or a television play of *A Proper Little Nooryeff*, yet more changes would be needed. The technology of film and video make quite different demands on the material. They also enable us to do things that are not possible through print or on the stage. You might like to think about the different conventions and write your own TV or film script for this play. Before you begin, you could look at the theatre and film scripts for *Gregory's Girl*[*] and note the differences of approach. For example, the scenes in the film script are often shorter and much more detailed. What are some of the other differences?

- Write your own film or video opening for *A Proper Little Nooryeff*. You may find it helpful to look at both the book and play versions. Remember, you don't need to stick strictly to either script.

Things to think about: –

– How do you quickly capture the mood of the piece? (Is it comic, tragic, realistic, phantasy etc.?)

---

[*] *Gregory's Girl* by Bill Forsyth is published as a playscript in the ACT NOW series and as a post-production film script edited by Paul Kelley. Both are Cambridge University Press publications.

- What technologies do you want to use other than the camera? (Sound / music / lighting / special effects?)
- How will the camera be used? Will it be like a fly on the wall, simply recording the activity or will you use the camera so that it records the activity from unusual angles or positions? What are you trying to achieve if you use the camera in these ways?
- What locations are you going to use for the scenes? Try and find actual locations and see if there are any drawbacks of special needs involved. For instance, if you are indoors, what are the lighting levels like and will you need extra sources of light?

If you have access to a video camera, it would be interesting then actually to shoot your opening scene. Don't worry if the quality of the video you make is less than you might have wanted. Remember, professional film and video makers work with considerable budgets, sophisticated technology and experienced, supporting staff, so their work can be expected to be more polished.

Having made your video, you may like to show it to an audience and discuss how it works or whether there are any improvements that could be made. How closely did you stick to your script? What changes were made? Why were they made?

ACT NOW PLAYS

Series editor: Peter Rowlands
Founding editor: Andrew Bethell

Roots, Rules and Tribulations Andrew Bethell
Closed Circuit Mike English
Faust and Furious Anne Lee
Gregory's Girl Bill Forsyth
Vacuees Bill Martin
Easy on the Relish Andrew Bethell
Wednesday's Child Tony Higgins
The Tree that Holds up the Sky Paul King
The Fourth Year are Animals Richard Tulloch
Do We Ever See Grace? Noël Greig
Rainbow's Ending Noël Greig
Kidsplay John Lee
Terms of Engagement Martin Dimery
Hard to Swallow Mark Wheeller
A Valuable Learning Experience Gillian Wadds
Heroin Lies Wayne Denfhy
Wolf Boy Peter Charlton
Dags Debra Oswald
A Nice Little Earner Arnold Evans
Clean Up Your Act Mike English
King of Limbo Adrian Flynn
Living with Lady Macbeth Rob John
Black Roses Steven Downs
The Fate of Jeremy Visick Judith Cook
A Proper Little Nooryeff Leonard Gregory